Coffee

A Guide for Using

Molly's Pilgrim

in the Classroom

Based on the novel written by Barbara Cohen

This guide written by **Susan Kilpatrick**

D1412106

Teacher Created Resources, Inc.
6421 Industry Way
Westminster, CA 92683
www.teachercreated.com

ISBN: 978-1-55734-535-6

©*1995 Teacher Created Resources, Inc.*
Reprinted, 2007
Made in U.S.A.

Teacher Created Resources

Edited by
Dona Herweck Rice

Illustrated by
Kathy Bruce

Cover Art by
Wendy Chang

Table of Contents

Introduction and Sample Lesson Plans

A good book can touch the lives of children like a good friend. Great care has been taken in selecting the books and activities featured in the *Literature Units* series. Teachers who use the activities here to supplement their own ideas can follow one of the following methods.

A Sample Lesson Plan

Each of the lessons suggested below can take from one to several days to complete and can include all or some of the suggested activities. Refer to pages 6–11 for additional information.

A Unit Planner

If you wish to tailor the suggestions on pages 6–11 in a format other than that prescribed in the plan below, use the "Unit Planner" on page 4. For any specific day, you may choose the activities you wish to include by writing the activity number or a brief notation about the lesson in the "unit activities" section. Space has also been provided for other related notes and comments. Reproduce copies of page 4 as needed.

Sample Lesson Plan

Lesson 1
Prepare the "Pocket Chart Activities" (pages 12-14).

Introduce the book by using some or all "Before the Book" activities (pages 6-7).

Read "About the Author" (page 5).

Discuss the new vocabulary (page 6).

Complete the "prior knowledge" side of the "Knowledge Chart" (page 22).

Prepare to read by completing activities 3, 5, and 6 on pages 6-7.

Read the book for enjoyment.

Complete the "new knowledge" side of the "Knowledge Chart" (page 22).

Lesson 2
Discuss the questions (page 15) to involve the students in critical thinking.

Use the sentence strips (page 16). Let the students sequence the story events.

Recite "A Pilgrim of Today" (page 17).

Complete "Main Idea" (page 26).

Begin practicing "Readers' Theater" (pages 43-46).

Learn "Pilgrim Song" (page 40).

Lesson 3
Recall the poem (page 17).

Complete "Open Mind" (pages 23-25). (Construct the cards to use beforehand.)

Prepare stick puppets and puppet theaters (pages 18-21). Use throughout the lessons to retell or review parts of the story.

Continue practicing the "Readers' Theater" (pages 43-46), the poem (page 17), and the song (page 40).

Lesson 4
Introduce "The Thanksgiving Game" (pages 31-35). Use the game throughout the unit.

Write letters to Molly (number 10, page 9).

Ask the students to talk to their parents about their ancestral heritage.

Continue practicing the "Readers' Theater" (pages 43-46), the poem (page 17), and the song (page 40).

Lesson 5
Complete "Where in the World Do Our Families Come From?" (page 36).

Complete "Schoolhouse Writing" (page 29).

Have the students construct and play "The Thanksgiving Game" (pages 31-35).

Lesson 6
Have the students construct "My November Turkey" (pages 27-28).

Complete "Following Directions" (page 30).

Continue practicing the "Readers' Theater" (pages 43-46), the poem (page 17), and the song (page 40).

Assign as homework the making of Pilgrim and Indian dolls (number 6, page 11).

Lesson 7
Complete "A Look at Corn" and "A Look at Popcorn" (pages 37-39).

Pop and enjoy some popcorn.

Make background scenes for the homemade dolls (number 6, page 11).

Make cornucopias to display (page 42).

Make and deliver culminating activity invitations (page 47).

Lesson 8
Prepare recipes (page 41) for a culminating program.

Host a culminating program (number 6, page 11).

Unit Planner

Unit Activities	Unit Activities
Date:	Date:
Notes/Comments	Notes/Comments
Unit Activities	Unit Activities
Date:	Date:
Notes/Comments	Notes/Comments
Unit Activities	Unit Activities
Date:	
Notes/Comments	Notes/Comments

Getting to Know the Book and Author

About the Book

(Available in U.S. by William Morrow; in Canada by Gage Distributors, in U.K. by International Book Distributors, and in Australia by Kirby Book Co.)

This heartwarming story is sure to touch the lives of children and adults. It tells of a young Jewish girl from Russia who moves to Winter Hill in the United States. There she encounters prejudice and intolerance.

Molly's classmates make fun of her accent and her clothes. She wants to go back to New York or even to return to Russia. However, the family's living conditions in their New York tenement were very poor, and Molly's mother reminds her of the Cossacks and danger in Russia.

For Thanksgiving, Molly's teacher, Miss Stickley, asks everyone to bring a Pilgrim doll to class. When Molly explains that a Pilgrim is "someone who came from the other side looking for religious freedom," Molly's mother makes a Russian peasant doll. Molly is worried because the doll does not look at all like the Pilgrims in her history book, and she is afraid the other children will laugh at her once more.

Her classmates do laugh at her at first, but Miss Stickley and Molly help the class learn the true meaning of Thanksgiving and that "it takes all kinds of pilgrims to make a Thanksgiving."

About the Author

Barbara Cohen is highly regarded for her adult novels as well as for her children's fiction. She has written several books about Jewish children, including *The Carp in the Bathtub*, which has been described by critics as a modern classic. Her books *The Christmas Revolution* and *The Orphan Game* are also about Jewish children.

In 1983, Mrs. Cohen received the National Jewish Book Award for children's fiction and was presented with the Sydney Taylor Body-of-Work Award by the Association of Jewish Librarians.

In 1986, the movie version of *Molly's Pilgrim* received an Academy Award for Best Short Film. It is available on video cassette and will delight everyone who has the opportunity to view it.

Mrs. Cohen lives in Bridgewater, New Jersey.

Suggestions for Using the Unit Activites

Use some or all of the following suggestions to introduce students to *Molly's Pilgrim* and to extend their appreciation of the book through activities that cross the curriculum.

The sections that follow are:

Before the Book: includes suggestions for preparing the classroom environment and the students for the literature to be read.

Into the Book: has activities that focus on the book's content, characters, and themes.

After the Book: extends the reader's enjoyment of the book.

Before the Book

1. **Preparation:** Before you begin the unit, prepare the vocabulary cards, story questions, and sentence strips for the pocket chart activities. (See samples, patterns, and directions on pages 12–16.)

2. **Themes:** Use *Molly's Pilgrim*, along with other stories and activities, to complete a unit on Thanksgiving. Explore such themes as "tolerance," "prejudice," "freedom," and "what it means to be an American."

3. **Background:** Set the stage for reading the book by asking the following questions and discussing the students' responses:

   • Have you ever been the "new student" in a school? How did you feel?

   • Have you known a student new to your school? How did you treat him or her?

   • What is the meaning of Thanksgiving today? What was its meaning at the time of the Pilgrims?

   • What is a Pilgrim? Are there any pilgrims today?

   • What is an American? How do you get to be an American?

   • If someone asked you to make a Pilgrim doll, what would it look like?

4. **Knowledge Chart:** Engage prior knowledge by asking the students to record what they already know about Pilgrims on the "Knowledge Chart" (page 22). The students should complete only the "prior knowledge" side of the chart at this time. The "new knowledge" side will be completed after they have read the story.

5. **Vocabulary:** Discuss the meaning of the following words before reading the story. Make several copies of the pumpkin pattern on page 14. Write one word on each pumpkin and display the pumpkins on a pocket chart. (See page 12 for directions on making a pocket chart.)

Jewish	synagogue	Yiddish (a blend of	*Shaynkeit* (pretty one)
modern	embroidered	German and Hebrew)	*Malkeleh* (little Molly)
tenement	taunted	*Oi* (Oh!)	Goraduk (Russian city)
ignorant	aisle	*paskudnyaks* (naughty	*Sukkos* (Jewish harvest
Russia	corkscrew curls	girls)	holiday)
		nu (so)	
		Cossack (Russian cavalry)	

Suggestions for Using the Unit Activites *(cont.)*

Before the Book *(cont.)*

6. **Geography:** Ask whether anyone knows where Russia is and locate it on a map. Also locate New York. Explain that the book does not tell us where Winter Hill is, except to say that it is within the United States.

7. **Using the Cover:** Display the cover of *Molly's Pilgrim*. Have the children look for clues that might convey the story setting and the approximate time period in which the story takes place.

8. **Personal Application:** Ask the students to try to put themselves in Molly's place as they listen to the story. Read the story to discover what happens to Molly in her new school.

Into the Book

1. **Story Questions:** Develop critical thinking skills with the story questions on page 15. The questions are based on Bloom's Taxonomy and are provided for each of Bloom's levels of learning. Reproduce several copies of the doll-shaped task card pattern on page 14 and write a story question on each doll. (See also pages 12 and 13.)

2. **Vocabulary:** Review the vocabulary words on page 6.

3. **Story Summary Sentence Strips:** Cut out and laminate the sentences on page 16 to use on a pocket chart. Complete some or all of the following activities.

   • On the pocket chart, sequence the sentences in the order in which the events happen in the story.

   • Use the sentences to retell the story.

   • Divide the class into small groups and distribute a few sentence strips to each group. Ask the groups to act out the part of the story to which the sentences refer.

   In addition to these activities, you may wish to reproduce page 16 and have the students read the sentences aloud to a partner or take them home to read to a parent, caretaker, or older sibling.

4. **Knowledge Chart:** Complete the "new knowledge" side of the "Knowledge Chart" (page 22). (See the sample responses below.)

Knowledge Chart	
Prior Knowledge	**New Knowledge**
1. came from England	1. come from many different countries
2. wore plain clothes, capes, and tall hats	2. wear many different kinds of clothing
3. spoke English	3. sometimes speak another language
4. were looking for religious freedom	4. are looking for a better way of life
5. came here on the *Mayflower*	5. come by foot, car, bus, plane, and boat
6. lived long ago	6. live today as well

Suggestions for Using the Unit Activites *(cont.)*

Into the Book *(cont.)*

5. **Stick Puppets and Puppet Theaters:** Prepare "Stick Puppet Theaters" following the suggestions and directions on page 18. Allow the students to construct puppets by coloring and cutting out the puppet patterns (pages 19-21) and gluing them to tongue depressors. Follow the suggestions at the bottom of page 18 for using the stick puppets.

6. **Open Mind:** Follow the directions on page 24 to construct the cards on pages 24-25. Use these cards to help students understand how others feel.

   Use the "Open Mind" figure on page 23 as a group writing activity. Allow the students to choose which character they will use. They can either draw the character or the teacher can reproduce the stick puppet figures and let the children color, cut out, and glue one in the empty space. The students will "get into" the character's mind and write from his or her point of view.

   The following samples may be used as models for the activity.

Open Mind of Molly: I wish we could go back to New York. I feel so bad when people tease me. I wish I could speak English better. I wish the other children liked me.

Open Mind of Mama: I am worried about Molly. She does not seem to be happy. I think I will go to school to talk with her teacher.

Open Mind of Miss Stickley: Molly is such a sweet, shy girl. I wonder how I can help her. I wish the other children would not make fun of her.

Open Mind of Elizabeth: Molly is so stupid. I can't believe that dumb Pilgrim she made! That song we sing about her is really funny.

7. **Main Idea:** Have the students distinguish between the main idea of the story and the story details. Instruct them to select the main idea and write it on the light bulb (page 26). See the example to the right.

A Pilgrim is someone who moves to a new place to find religious freedom.

8

Suggestions for Using the Unit Activites *(cont.)*

Into the Book *(cont.)*

8. **My November Turkey:** Use this project to create a bulletin board reinforcing a variety of skills. Display the caption "Our November Turkeys." Some skills to be used include:

   - sequencing ABC order
   - giving one's name and address (turn feathers sideways)
   - completing math problems
   - counting by 2s (5s, 10s, etc.)
   - naming the days of the week
   - giving dictionary definitions (from *Molly's Pilgrim* vocabulary)
   - writing root words
   - circling prefixes and suffixes

9. **Schoolhouse Writing:** Help students put themselves in the place of a new student with this activity. The students can think of ways they can make a child new to the class feel welcome. See the directions on page 29 for additional information. Display the completed schoolhouse stories.

10. **Letter Writing:** Ask the students whether they know what it means to be tolerant and accepting of others (and whether they possess these qualities). Discuss the concepts of tolerance and acceptance.

    Then, encourage the students to talk about how their families celebrate Thanksgiving. As they brainstorm with you, write their responses in the following sections on the chalkboard:
    A. What do you eat? (examples: turkey, stuffing, corn)
    B. Where do you go? (examples: relatives' house, church, stay home)
    C. With whom do you celebrate? (examples: grandparents, aunts, uncles, cousins)
    D. Why do Americans celebrate Thanksgiving, and what are they thankful for? (examples: food, shelter, friends, family, country, school)

    Next, ask students to write a letter to Molly inviting her to their homes for Thanksgiving. (Tell them to include the information listed in A, B, C, and D above). End with a request to Molly that she relate something about one of her religious holidays. Be sure to review and use the proper form for a friendly letter, including a greeting, body, and closing.

    As an extension, write letters to another class, to another school, to relatives, or to friends in other states. Have the students share aloud any replies they receive.

    Here is a sample letter to share with the students.

November 15, 1996

Dear Molly,
I would like to invite you and your family to visit my home on Thanksgiving Day. We will have a big feast of turkey, stuffing, corn, cranberry sauce, and pumpkin pie. My grandparents are coming to visit as well.
Thanksgiving is a special holiday. We think about the things we are grateful for, such as our food, family, home, friends, school, and country. I will tell you more about Thanksgiving when you come. Will you tell me about one of your special holidays?

Your friend,
Emily Williams

Suggestions for Using the Unit Activites *(cont.)*

After the Book

1. **Following Directions:** The students will enjoy reading and drawing as they complete the activity on page 30. Encourage them to read carefully and be sure their pictures are accurate.

2. **The Thanksgiving Game:** This game is a social studies activity and can be found on pages 31–35. Construct one or two class copies of the game. If possible, laminate all pieces. Students will enjoy playing the game, and while doing so, they will be reinforcing what they have learned about this historic event.

   Show students how to construct their own copies of the game. After using them during class for a day or two, allow the students to take their games home to play with a parent or sibling.

3. **Where in the World Do Our Families Come From?:** This is a graphing activity and can be found on page 36. Have the students ask their parents about their ethnic backgrounds and from which countries they or their ancestors originally came. Use a world map to locate the countries. Make a large class graph as a model and let the students complete their own small graph. This is a good opportunity to talk about America as a melting pot or as a salad bowl (as it is commonly referred to today). Build pride in the students with regard to their own ethnic backgrounds as well as their importance to the whole. This is also an excellent opportunity to discuss tolerance, prejudice, and acceptance of all people regardless of race or religion.

4. **A Look at Corn:** Before using page 37 (a science activity), ask the students if they can guess which four crops are the most important in the world today. (The answers are corn, wheat, rice, and potatoes.) Without Squanto's help in teaching the Pilgrims how to plant corn, it is believed the first colony of Pilgrims may not have survived.

   Ask the students to see how many corn products they can name. Let them work with partners to complete the bottom of page 37. (Corn products include corn flakes, taco shells, tortillas, corn chips, corn bread, popcorn, corn syrup, catsup, chewing gum, tamales, margarine, salad dressing, sausage, ice cream, jams and jellies, and many more. These are only food products. Use the encyclopedia to discover other products that contain corn.)

5. **A Look at Popcorn:** Popcorn, has been around for thousands of years. Help the students discover exactly how popcorn pops by using the science and math activities on pages 38 and 39. You may also wish to watch some popcorn popping and then, of course, enjoy eating it.

Suggestions for Using the Unit Activites *(cont.)*

After the Book *(cont.)*

6. **Culminating Activities:** Celebrate the literature unit with a day of enjoyment for students, teachers, and parents. Use the following activities and ideas for your culminating celebration.

   a. **Reader's Theater:** Have the students present the "Readers' Theater" production (pages 43–46). Send student-made invitations (or page 47) to other classes, teachers, and parents. Suggestions for implementing a readers' theater format are provided on page 43.

   b. **Poetry:** Reproduce the poem, "A Pilgrim of Today" (page 17). Divide the class into four groups and assign each group a verse of the poem. Have the groups choral read and act out their verses. As part of the culminating activities, assign a student or small group of students to recite each verse at the close of the "Readers' Theater" production. For additional poems, refer to any number of available children's anthologies.

   c. **Music:** Reproduce "Pilgrim Song" on page 40. Practice the music and lyrics with the class. Have the class sing "Pilgrim Song" following the poetry reading. You may also wish to sing "Over the River and Through the Woods" or other holiday favorites.

   d. **Thanksgiving Recipes:** Prepare recipes for corn muffins, cranberry relish, and no-bake pumpkin pies (page 41). You may wish to serve apple juice with these recipes. Serve this minifeast to guests and performers following the previous productions.

   e. **Cornucopias:** Using the cornucopia pattern and directions on page 42, gather the necessary materials and guide the students as they construct their cornucopias. Display on a wall for visiting parents and classes to see.

   f. **Dolls and Backdrop:** Explain to the students that they can make Pilgrim and Indian clothespin dolls just like the ones in the book. Have the students also construct a three-sided, illustrated backdrop for the dolls. Display the clothespin figures and other mini-props in front of the backdrop.

Pocket Chart Activities

Prepare a pocket chart for sorting and using the vocabulary cards, the story question cards, and the sentence strips.

How to Make a Pocket Chart

If a commercial pocket chart is unavailable, you can make a pocket chart if you have access to a laminator. Begin by laminating a 24" x 36" (60 cm x 90 cm) piece of colored tagboard. Run about 20" (50 cm) of additional plastic. To make nine pockets, cut the clear plastic into nine equal strips. Space the strips equally down the 36" (90 cm) length of the tagboard. Attach each strip with cellophane tape along the bottom and sides. This will hold sentence strips, word cards, and so forth. The chart can be displayed in a learning center or mounted on a chalk tray for use with a group. When your pocket chart is ready, use it to display the sentence strips, vocabulary words, and question cards. A sample chart is provided below.

---

taunted	modern	tenement	Russia	Cossack	ignorant

Molly wanted to leave Winter Hill because the other children in her class made fun of her.	Knowledge
Her family could not go back to New York. They had lived in a tenement there. Her father had a better job in Winter Hill.	Comprehension
Molly's family could not get back to Russia. The Cossacks had burned their synagogue.	Application
Molly tried to make the best of things.	Analysis
Miss Stickley asked the children to make clothespin dolls.	Synthesis

---

How to Use the Pocket Chart

1. On blue construction or index paper, reproduce the pumpkin and doll patterns on page 14. Make vocabulary cards as directed on page 6. (You may wish to include the chapter in which the word appears.) To familiarize the children with difficult words and their meanings, present the vocabulary cards for each chapter before reading the corresponding chapters. Help students understand the word meanings by providing context clues.

The patterns can also be used to make "Amazing Author," "Wonderful Work," "Great Reader," and other appropriate awards or incentives.

Pocket Chart Activities *(cont.)*

How to Use the Pocket Chart (cont.)

2. Reproduce several copies of the doll pattern (page 14) on six different colors of construction paper. Use a different paper color to represent each of Bloom's Levels of Learning.

   For example:

   I.   Knowledge (green)

   II. Comprehension (pink)

   III. Application (lavender)

   IV. Analysis (orange)

   V.   Synthesis (blue

   VI. Evaluation (yellow)

   Comprehension:

   Why did Molly's family leave New York?

   Write a story question from page 15 on the appropriate color-coded doll. Write the level of the question, the question itself, and the chapter section on the body of the doll as shown in the example.

   Use the doll-shaped cards after the corresponding chapters have been read to provide opportunities for the students to develop and practice higher level critical thinking skills. The cards can be used with some or all of the following activities.

   • Use a specific color-coded set of cards to question students at a particular level of learning.

   • Have a student choose a card, read it aloud, or give it to the teacher to read aloud. The student answers the question or calls on a volunteer to answer it.

   • Pair the students. The teacher reads a question. The students take turns with their partners responding to the question.

   • Play a game. Divide the class into teams. Ask for a response to a question written on one of the question cards. The teams score a point for each apppropriate response. If question cards have been prepared for several different stories, mix up the cards and ask the team members to respond by naming the story that relates to the question. Extra points can be awarded if a team member answers the question as well.

3. Use the sentence strips to practice oral reading and sequencing of the story events. Reproduce page 16. If possible, laminate the sentence strips for durability. Cut out the sentence strips or prepare sentences of your own to use with the pocket chart.

Pocket Chart Patterns

See pages 6, 12, and 13 for directions.

Story Questions

I. Knowledge

1. Who is Miss Stickley?

2. Which holiday customs were the students studying?

3. Molly's family originally came from what country?

4. What is a Cossack?

II. Comprehension

1. What assignment did the teacher, Miss Stickley, give to the students?

2. Why did Molly's family leave New York?

3. Why did Molly's family leave Russia?

III. Application

1. If Miss Stickley asked you to make a Pilgrim, how would it be different from Molly's doll? How might it be the same?

2. How did you feel when you read (or heard) about the girls taunting Molly?

3. Predict what will happen if Molly's mother comes to visit her class.

IV. Analysis

1. How was Molly's doll different from the other students' dolls?

2. Are "ignorant" and "stupid" the same thing?

3. Can you be ignorant and intelligent at the same time?

4. Explain the meaning of "May they (the Cossacks) grow like onions, with their heads in the ground."

V. Synthesis

1. What can you tell your classmates about the country or countries from which your family originally came?

2. What can you do to make someone new to your school feel welcome?

VI. Evaluation

1. Why is Miss Stickley a good teacher?

2. Why is it important to understand other people's feelings and respect the things they believe in?

3. Are you more like Molly or Elizabeth? Explain.

Story Summary Sentence
Strips

See page 7 for directions.

Molly wanted to leave Winter Hill because the children in her class made fun of her.
Molly's family could not return to New York. They had lived in a tenement there. Molly's father had a better job in Winter Hill.
Molly's family could not go back to Russia. The Cossacks had burned their synagogue.
Molly tried to make the best of things.
Miss Stickley asked the children to make clothespin dolls.
Molly's mother made a beautiful Russian pilgrim out of cloth, stuffing, and yarn.
The children in Molly's class laughed at her pilgrim.
Miss Stickley explained that all people who come to a place to find freedom are pilgrims.

A Pilgrim of Today

A pilgrim leaves his homeland

With many thoughts in mind.

Freedom is the first thing

He's hoping he will find.

It isn't always easy

To begin your life anew,

In a land where no one speaks

Exactly the same as you.

So when you meet a pilgrim,

A person from far away,

Hold out your hand and smile,

Tell him, "I hope you'll stay."

And be proud that America

Offers the chance to be free,

And welcomes pilgrims of today,

People just like you and me.

—Susan Kilpatrick

Stick Puppet Theaters

Make a class set of puppet theaters (one per student) or make one theater for every two to four students.

Materials: 22" x 28" (56 cm x 71 cm) pieces of colored poster board (enough for each student or group of students); markers, crayons, or paints; scissors or craft knife (used by an adult)

Directions:

1. Fold the poster board about 8" (20 cm) in from each of the shorter sides.

2. Cut a window in the center of the theater, large enough to accommodate two or three puppets. (See the illustration.)

3. Let the children personalize and decorate their own theaters.

4. Laminate the theaters to make them more durable. You may wish to send the theaters home at the end of the year or save them to use year after year.

Suggestions for Using the Puppets and Puppet Theaters:

• Prepare the stick puppets, using the directions on page 8. Use the puppets and puppet theaters with the "Readers' Theater" script on pages 44-46. (Let small groups of children take turns reading the parts and using the stick puppets.)

• Let children experiment with the puppets by telling the story in their own words.

• Read quotations from the book or make statements about the characters and ask students to hold up the stick puppets represented by the quotes or statements.

Stick Puppet Patterns

Molly

Elizabeth

Hilda

Kitty

Stick Puppet Patterns *(cont.)*

Miss Stickley

Mama

Emma

Faye

Stick Puppet Patterns *(cont.)*

Extension: Give each student a piece of white construction paper to design a background scene from the story. Then, tell the children to arrange and glue down the puppet figures without sticks. The students can add speech bubbles (below) and write something for each character to say.

Name _____

Date _____

Knowledge Chart

Prior Knowledge About Pilgrims

1.

2.

3.

4.

5.

6.

New Knowledge About Pilgrims

1.

2.

3.

4.

5.

6.

Name_____ Date_____

Open Mind

Draw a character from *Molly's Pilgrim* in the empty space or color and cut out one of the stick puppet patterns and glue it there. Write the name of the character in the blank space below the head pattern. For additional directions, see number 6 on page 8. Also refer to page 24.

Character's name_____ .

Open Mind *(cont.)*

1. Ask the students what kind of pilgrims Molly and her mother were.

2. Read the poem on page 17, "A Pilgrim of Today." Discuss the possible feelings of a modern pilgrim.

3. Ask the students what might be in the mind of someone leaving home to travel to a new place. Suggest that they envision themselves in the other person's place.

4. Show the students the "Open Mind" pattern on page 23. Model sample responses that might be made by the four main characters in *Molly's Pilgrim* (Molly, Mama, Elizabeth, and Miss Stickley) and elicit examples from the students. (See page 8, number 6)

5. Direct the students to work in collaborative pairs, groups, or individually to complete at least one "Open Mind" paper.

6. After the students have had time to work, let them share their ideas orally as a whole-class group. Note the differences and similarities in their responses.

7. Use the cards below and on the next page. Cut them out, glue them to colored construction paper squares, and laminate them. Write your own cards in the empty spaces. (The cards on this page reflect the thoughts of characters from *Molly's Pilgrim*. The cards on the next page are for real people and characters from other stories.)

Ask the students to put themselves in someone else's mind to try to figure out who is talking and how each person is feeling. You might select students to come forward and choose a card, read it aloud, and call on someone else to suggest who is talking and how that person is feeling.

(Mama)	(Miss Stickley)	(Molly)
I worry so much about Molly. She does not seem very happy. I love her so much.	I don't like it at all when the other children tease Molly. I wonder if I should speak with their parents.	Maybe it won't be so bad here. I think I'll be able to make some friends here after all.

(Elizabeth)	(Molly)	(Miss Stickley)
I don't like Molly because she is so different. Too bad she can't be more like us.	I hope I am not asked to read aloud. Everyone will laugh at me.	I am going to put this beautiful doll right where everyone can see it. It will remind us that pilgrims are still coming to America today.

(Molly)	(Mama)	(Elizabeth)
I wish I didn't have to stay in a place where no one likes me.	Pilgrims are people who come from the other side to find freedom. I am a Pilgrim!	I can't believe how stupid that new girl is. Did you see her Pilgrim?

Open Mind (cont.)

(librarian) Room 2 is coming to see me today. I hope they all remember to return their books.	(Peter Rabbit) I'm so glad I finally got out of there! I don't know what mother will say when she finds out I lost my jacket in Mr. McGregor's garden.	
(parent) I hope my child comes straight home after school. I worry when he (or she) is late.	(Max in *Where the Wild Things Are*) I wonder who those strange beasts are. They keep roaring terrible roars and rolling their terrible yellow eyes.	
(teacher) Wouldn't it be nice if everyone brought his or her homework back on time this week?	(Alexander in *Alexander and the Terrible, Horrible, No Good, Very Bad Day*) I hate lima beans, kissing on TV, my railroad train pajamas, and white sneakers. I'm moving to Australia.	
(principal) I am very proud of this school. I like to visit all the classes and see what everyone is doing.		
(Little Red Hen) Sometimes it makes me angry that I have to do everything all by myself. It isn't fair that no one helped me plant the wheat or make it into bread.		

Write your own cards in the blanks. Make them unique to your own class or use stories your class has read.

Main Idea

Directions: Read the sentences below. Which is the main idea of *Molly's Pilgrim*? Write it on the light-bulb.

1. The "First Thanksgiving" took place in Plymouth, Massachusetts.

2. Molly and her family came to America from Russia.

3. Molly does not like being teased by the other children.

4. A pilgrim is someone who moves to a new place to find religious freedom.

5. Miss Stickley is a kind, understanding teacher.

Title: _____

By: _____

My November Turkey

Make copies of the turkey below on brown construction paper. Give one to each student. See the next page and page 9, number 8, for additional directions.

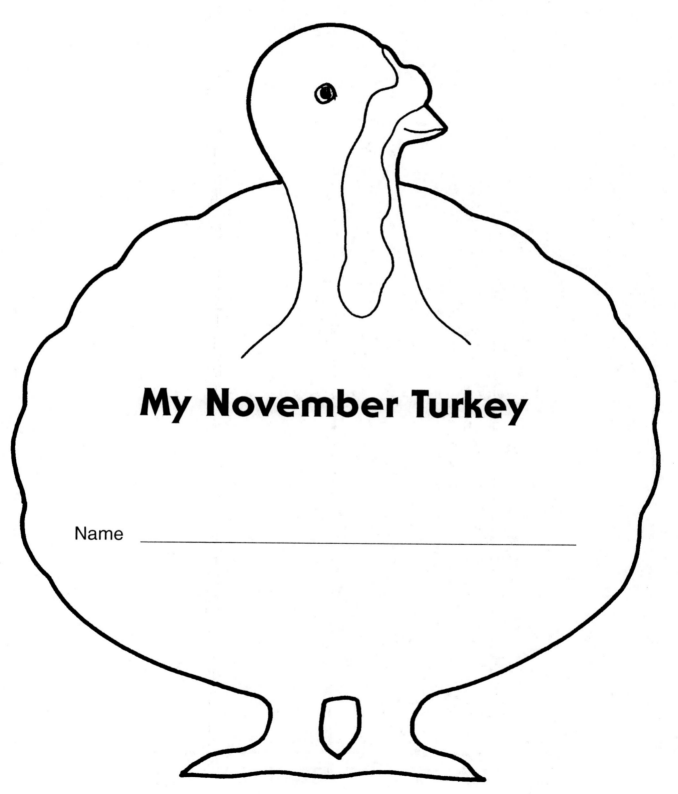

My November Turkey

Name _____

My November Turkey *(cont.)*

Make six to nine copies of this page. Select skills you would like to reinforce. (See the ideas on page 9, number 8.) Fill in the feathers with only one skill per page. (The four feathers on each page should be identical.) Copy (or photocopy) the feathers in fall colors such as yellow, orange, red, and green. The children can complete the feathers, have them corrected, cut them out, and attach them to the turkey on page 27 with a brad. (The feathers go behind the turkey.)

When complete, display the turkeys on a bulletin board with the heading, "Our November Turkeys."

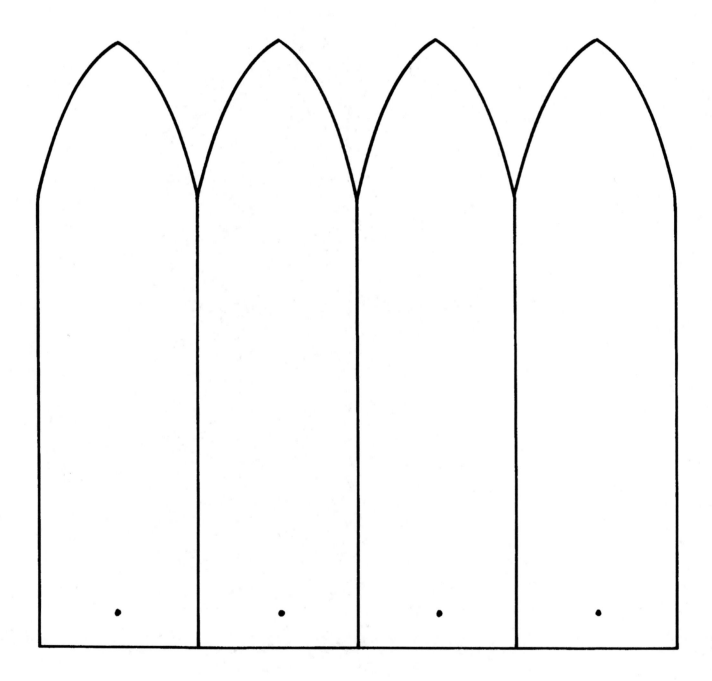

Schoolhouse Writing

1. Cut out the schoolhouse shape. Place the long edge on a fold of red construction paper. Trace the pattern and cut it out. Open the paper to have a complete schoolhouse.

2. Staple lined writing paper to a ¼ sheet of red construction paper.

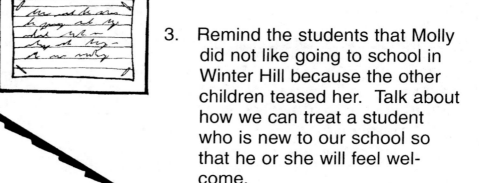

3. Remind the students that Molly did not like going to school in Winter Hill because the other children teased her. Talk about how we can treat a student who is new to our school so that he or she will feel welcome.

4. Have the students write their own compositions on welcoming new students to their school. Have them begin in this way:

   There are several things I can do to make a new student feel welcome. I can…

5. Staple the schoolhouse to the story along the lefthand side.

6. Draw in a door and windows.

7. Open like a book to read.

Place on fold (red construction paper)

Following Directions

1. Fold a large sheet of white construction paper or drawing paper into eight sections. (Your teacher will show you how.)

2. Number each section.

3. In section 1, draw an orange pumpkin, a green apple, and a yellow banana. Write your name three times.

4. In section 2, draw a fat turkey. Give him one yellow, two red, three green, and four orange feathers.

5. In section 3, draw a picture of the *Mayflower* on the ocean.

6. In section 4, draw a Pilgrim man and a Pilgrim woman.

7. In section 5, draw two clouds, four birds, a rainbow, and a purple kite.

8. In section 6, draw some grass, five flowers, an airplane, and an orange car.

9. In section 7, draw a tree with seven red apples. Put a house next to the tree.

10. In section 8, draw yourself. Put a funny hat on your head, a balloon in one hand, and an ice cream cone in the other hand.

11. On the back of this paper, draw a large cornucopia. Fill it with at least six kinds of fruits and vegetables.

12. Staple this paper to the back of your artwork. Check to be sure you have followed all directions.

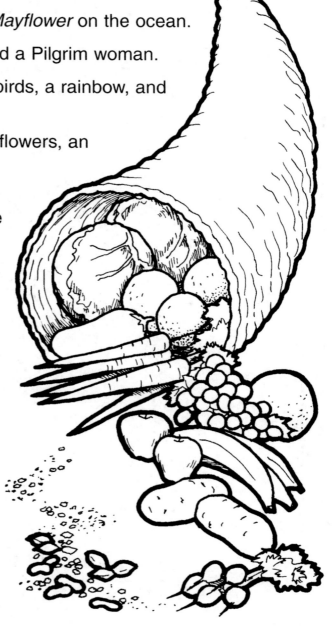

The Thanksgiving Game

The Pilgrims set sail
Across the wide sea
To a land called America
Where they could be free.

— *Susan Kilpatrick*

To construct a class copy of the game, color, cut out, and glue the pattern above to a large manila envelope. Glue the answer sheet (page 33) to the back. Laminate.

To construct a student copy of the game, have each student color and cut out the pattern above and glue it to the front of a construction paper folder.

See page 10 (number 2) and pages 32–35 for additional directions and game pieces.

The Thanksgiving Game *(cont.)*

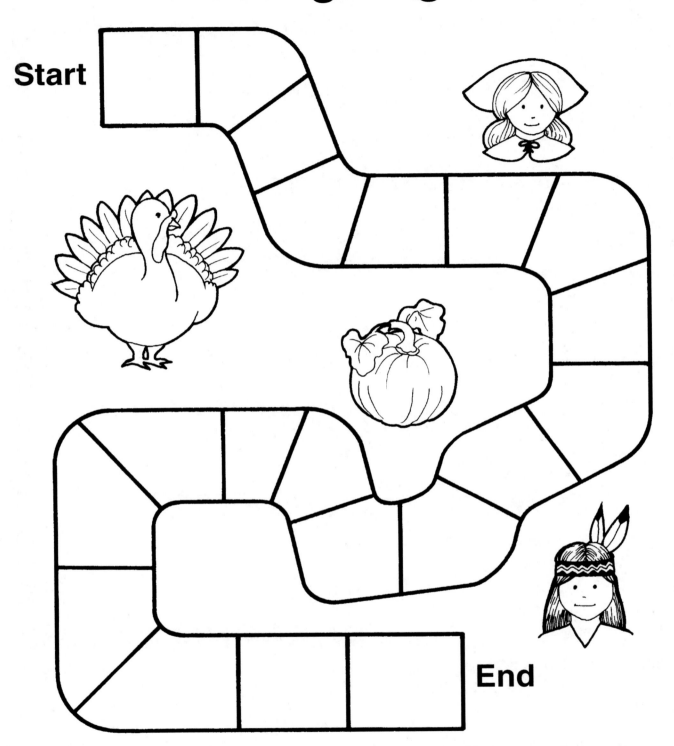

Start

End

For the class copy, color and cut out the pattern above. Glue it to a ¹/₂ sheet of colored construction paper. Laminate it and store it inside the large envelope.

For the student copies, have the students each color and cut out the pattern above. They can then glue it inside their construction paper folders.

The Thanksgiving Game (cont.)

Game Directions:

This game is for 2, 3, or 4 players. Each player will need a marker. Use a die or a spinner.

To play, place the task cards (pages 34 and 35) face down in a pile. The first player takes a task card and answers the question. If the answer is correct, the player may roll the die (or spin the spinner) and move that many spaces. If the answer is incorrect, the player stays on the same space until his or her next turn. The first player to reach the end wins.

- For the class copy, cut out and glue the directions above to a 1/2 sheet of colored construction paper.
- For the student copies, have the students each cut out and glue the directions above inside his or her construction paper folder.

Answer Sheet:

1. England
2. Holland
3. *Mayflower* and *Speedwell*
4. It sprang a leak and had to return to England.
5. Atlantic
6. 102
7. mostly dried meat and hard biscuits
8. seasickness, poor food, or cold and wet
9. to find religious freedom
10. 66 days
11. Plymouth Colony
12. Chief Massasoit
13. Many of the Pilgrims became sick and died.
14. Samoset and Squanto
15. how to plant corn, where to fish, or how to hunt for food
16. live in peace and be friends
17. They were thankful for the harvest.
18. 3 days
19. hunt, fish, dig for clams, or catch lobsters
20. prepare food, carry water, make candles, gather wood, or do the spinning
21. a person who travels to a far-off place to find religious freedom

- For the class copy, cut out, laminate, and glue the answer sheet above to the back of the large envelope.
- For the student copies, have each student cut out the answer sheet above and glue it to the back of his or her construction paper folder.

The Thanksgiving Game (cont.)

Task Cards:

1. What country did the Pilgrims leave?	2. Where did the Pilgrims go for awhile before they came to America?	3. What were the names of the Pilgrims' two ships?
4. What happened to one of the Pilgrims' ships?	5. What ocean did the Pilgrims cross?	6. How many passengers sailed on the *Mayflower*?
7. What did the Pilgrims eat while they were on the ship?	8. Give one reason why so many people were sick while on the ship.	9. Why did the Pilgrims want to come to America?
10. How long did it take to sail to America on the *Mayflower*?	11. What was the name of the Pilgrim settlement in America?	12. What was the name of the Indian chief the Pilgrims met?
13. What happened during the first winter?	14. Name two Indians who were of great help to the Pilgrims.	15. Name one thing Squanto taught the Pilgrims.
16. What did the Indians and the Pilgrims agree to do?	17. Give one reason why the Pilgrims wanted to have a big feast.	18. How long did the First Thanksgiving last?

The Thanksgiving Game *(cont.)*

Task Cards *(cont.)*:

19. Name two things the Pilgrim boys learned to do.	20. Name two things the Pilgrim girls learned to do.	21. What is a Pilgrim?

- For the class copy, cut out the task cards above and on the previous page. Glue an envelope below the game directions card (page 33) on the same sheet of construction paper. Laminate it, but first be sure the flap is open. Put the task cards inside the envelope. Store everything in the large manila envelope.

- For the student copies, have each student cut out the task cards above and on the previous page and then place them in an envelope. They can then glue the envelope inside their folders. To keep the cards from being lost, you might also duplicate copies of the hat pattern below, glue the task cards to them, and laminate them. The task cards will still fit in the envelope, but they will not be so easy to lose.

Name _____

Date _____

Where in the World Do Our Families Come From?

See additional directions on page 10, number 3.

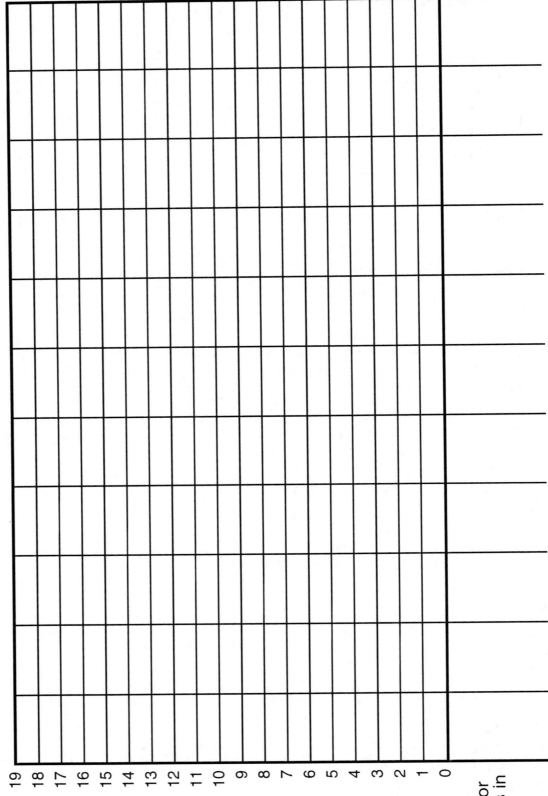

19												
18												
17												
16												
15												
14												
13												
12												
11												
10												
9												
8												
7												
6												
5												
4												
3												
2												
1												
0												

Write in countries or continents in these spaces.

A Look at Corn

How important is corn?

Where did corn originate?

What products are made from corn?

Corn is the most valuable crop in the United States today, and it is one of the four most important crops in the world (along with wheat, rice, and potatoes).

Corn is native to North America. No one in Europe knew about corn until Columbus came to America in 1492. Early explorers discovered that Indians were growing corn in Canada and all the way down to the tip of South America.

Squanto taught the Pilgrims to plant corn (and pumpkins and beans) by using fish as a fertilizer. It is believed that Plymouth Colony might have failed if Squanto had not taught the Pilgrims how to plant crops (especially corn) and where to fish.

After you answer the three questions at the top of the page, see how many products you can think of that are made from corn. Write the name of the product on the line and then draw a picture in the box.

Teacher Note: See page 10 for a list of corn products.

A Look at Popcorn

Popcorn, one variety of corn, has been around for a very long time. Thousands of years ago, Indian children in the Tehuacan Valley in Mexico popped corn. Today, it is one of the most popular snack foods in America.

All corn kernels have starch in them. They have a little water in them, too. But popcorn kernels have thick, tough outer coats. When you heat popcorn kernels, the water inside turns to steam. The steam expands and starts to push against the tough outer coats. The hotter the steam gets, the more it pushes. Soon the kernels explode, and you suddenly see the white, fluffly starch.

Heat   **Steam builds up**   **Pop!**
                                                                That is how popcorn pops!

Things to Do:

1. Watch popcorn kernels sprout and grow by planting them in an egg carton. Put some planting mix (or good soil) and 3 or 4 popcorn kernels into each section of an egg carton. Keep the soil moist. While you wait, make some predictions:

   A. I think it will take _____ days before the first sprout appears.

   B. I think the tallest sprout will grow to be _____ inches/centimeters high.

   Follow through with your predictions. What actually happened?

   A. It actually took _____ days before the first sprout appeared.

   B. The tallest sprout actually grew to be _____ inches/centimeters high.

2. Popcorn should pop in one minute if the popcorn is fresh. One cup (250 mL) of corn should give you 30 cups (7.5 L) of popcorn. Using this information, complete the following:

Kernels of Corn	Popped Corn
2 cups (500 mL)	=
3 cups (750 mL)	=
4 cups (1 L)	=
5 cups (1.25 L)	=
6 cups (1.5 L)	=

A Look at Popcorn *(cont.)*

Things to Do *(cont.)*

3. Conduct a popcorn taste test. Pop equal amounts of three different brands
   of popcorn. Take a class vote and record the results.

Brand A   **Brand B**   **Brand C**

_____   _____   _____

(_____)   (_____)   (_____)

Popcorn Graph

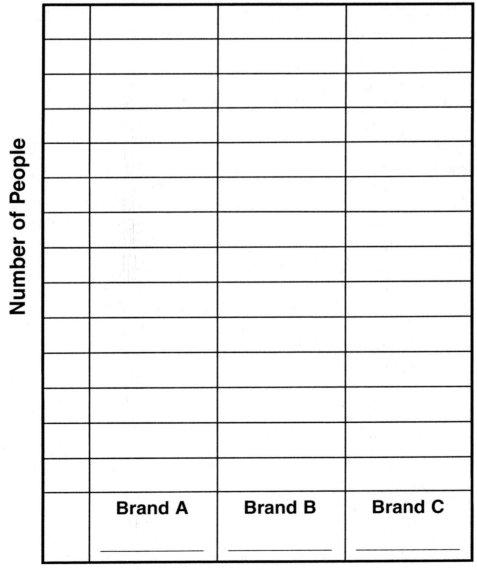

Pilgrim Song

Words and Music by Mary E. Hicks. Used with permission.

When I hear the Thanksgiving story of old,
Pilgrims set sail for freedom or worship I'm told.
It's surprising to me that their feelings I know,
My voyage is beginning and I have far yet to go.

Chorus:
> 'Cause we all still are pilgrims,
> And we carry our load.
> Life is a journey,
> Learning, our road.
> Flooded with memories
> From the places we've come,
> Laughing and loving
> We find our way home.

Pilgrims still come from many far distant lands,
Looking for freedom and work for their hands.
Do we welcome them here or just turn them away?
Open your hearts and give them reasons to stay.

Thanksgiving Recipes

Corn Muffins

Ingredients:

- 1 cup (250 mL) milk
- 1 egg
- 1 cup (250 mL) flour
- ⅓ cup (85 mL) sugar
- 1 cup (250 mL) yellow cornmeal
- ¼ cup (65 mL) soft margarine
- 1 tbsp. (15 mL) baking powder

Preparation:

Sift flour and baking powder together. Mix in milk and egg. Add the remaining ingredients.
Bake in well-greased muffin tins at 425° F (220° C). Yields one dozen muffins.

Cranberry Relish

Ingredients:

- 1 package cranberries
- 1 medium-sized orange
- ½-¾ cup (125-180 mL) sugar

Preparation:

Chop the cranberries and unpeeled orange in a food processor or grinder. Add sugar for
desired sweetness. Refrigerate or serve at once with the muffins.

No-Bake Pumpkin Pies

Ingredients for One Small Pie Crust:

- 1 whole graham cracker, crushed
- 1 heaping tsp. (5 mL) sugar
- 1 tbsp. (15 mL) liquid margarine

Ingredients for One Filling:

- 1½ cups (375 mL) milk
- 1 small package instant vanilla pudding
- 1 cup (250 mL) canned pumpkin filling
- 1 tsp. (5 mL) pumpkin spice
- whipped cream

Preparation:

Pat the crust ingredients together into a foil muffin cup. Beat the filling ingredients for one
minute. Spoon it into the muffin cup. Refrigerate for one hour. Top with whipped cream.

Cornucopia

Cornucopia Pattern

1. Trace the cornucopia pattern onto brown construction paper. Cut it out.

2. Shape the cut paper into a cone. Staple it together.

3. Glue the cornucopia (stapled side down) onto a 1/2 sheet of white construction paper.

4. Fold another sheet of white construction paper into 8 sections.

5. The teacher draws on the chalkboard while the students draw on their papers the following fruit and vegetable shapes:

6. The students outline the fruit shapes in black crayon and then fill in with watercolors. When the painting is dry, they can cut out the fruit shapes and glue them to the paper so that they are coming out of the cornucopia.

Readers' Theater

Readers' theater is an exciting and easy method of providing students with the opportunity to perform a play while minimizing the use of props, sets, costumes, or memorization. Students read the dialogue of the characters, narrator, chorus, and so forth, from a book or prepared script. The dialogue may be verbatim from the book, or an elaboration may be written by the performing students. Sound effects and dramatic voices can make these much like radio plays.

In a reader's theater production, everyone in the class can be involved in some way. The thirteen speaking parts in this reader's theater, in addition to the poem on page 17 and the song on page 40, maximize student involvement. Encourage class members to participate in off-stage activities as well, such as greeting the audience and assisting behind the scenes.

It is not necessary to wear costumes for a readers' theater production, but the students can wear signs around their necks indicating their speaking parts. Prepare signs by writing the reader's character on a piece of construction paper. Laminate it, if possible, for durability. Then, staple a necklace-length piece of yarn to the top of the paper (or punch holes and tie with yarn).

Prepare script booklets for the readers as well. It is well worth the time, and you will have them to use again and again. You will need one script booklet for each reader, including the announcer, the narrator, and the teacher. Highlight (with yellow marking pen) all lines spoken by an individual reader. Write the title and author of the piece being read as well as the name of the character being highlighted on the outside cover of the booklet. Laminate the cover for durability, and then glue (do not staple) the pages of the script into the booklet.

For a 2–3 page script, construct the booklet as follows:

For a 3–6 page script, construct the booklet as follows:

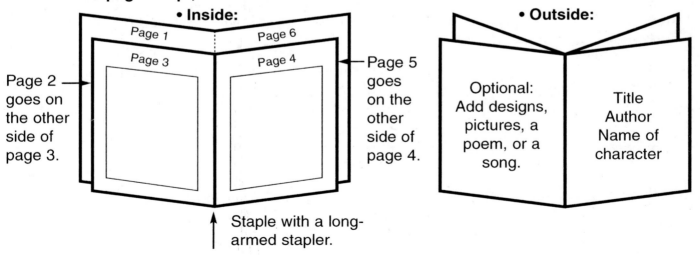

The Thanksgiving Program

By Susan Kilpatrick

Announcer: Welcome to our Readers Theater presentation of "The Thanksgiving Program." Our readers are as follows:

Announcer	*Jeff*	*Sima*
Narrator 1	*Ben*	*Andy*
Narrator 2	*Lisa*	*Karen*
Narrator 3	*Mai Li*	*Nicholas*
Mrs. O'Connor	*Mario*	

Narrator 1: Our story takes place in an ordinary classroom somewhere in the U.S.A.

Narrator 2: The teacher, Mrs. O'Connor, is helping the class plan a Thanksgiving program.

Narrator 3: The children have already decided they want to invite their parents, the class next door, and the principal, too.

Narrator 1: But they can't decide what kind of program to have.

Mrs. O'Connor: Thanksgiving is next week, class. We have to start practicing soon. Doesn't anyone have an idea of what we can do to entertain our guests?

Jeff: Well, we could have a play and wear costumes, but don't ask me to dress up like a turkey!

Ben: Speaking of turkey, I think we should have a huge Thanksgiving feast . . . and that reminds me, isn't it about time for lunch?

Lisa: Stop thinking about food, and let's get serious. We're running out of time.

Mrs. O'Connor: It might be a good idea to serve some food. I have a delicious recipe for no-bake pumpkin pie, but we have to decide what we will do first.

Mai Li: We could sing songs and recite poems. Remember "The Pilgrim Song" we learned yesterday?

Sima: That's a good idea. I love to sing, and we already know a poem called "A Pilgrim of Today."

The Thanksgiving Program (cont.)

Andy: I think we should tell our parents what we've learned about the first Thanksgiving.

Karen: We could tell them about the difficult trip to America on the *Mayflower*.

Nicholas: We could dress up like Pilgrims and Indians and tell them about life in Plymouth Colony.

Ben: And we could end it all with a three-day feast just like the first Thanksgiving!

Jeff: Don't forget to say why the Pilgrims had a feast. They wanted to give thanks for the good harvest.

Andy: I want to be Squanto and show the Pilgrims how to plant corn and catch fish.

Mario: Could I be Chief Massasoit and sign the peace treaty for the Indians?

Ben: I'd like to be Governor Bradford and sign the treaty for the Pilgrims.

Mai Li: I could be a Pilgrim woman and tell how to make candles and cook over an open fire.

Lisa: Well, I think only people who are real Americans should get to be the Pilgrims and the Indians.

Sima: What's a real American, Lisa? I don't understand.

Lisa: Someone who was born in America, not someone who came here from another country . . . and I think the parents of real Americans were born here, too.

Jeff: Wow! You must not have been listening when we learned about the Pilgrims.

Karen: You can say that again! The Pilgrims themselves came here from another country . . . England.

Mai Li: They were looking for a better way of life. America became their country.

Nicholas: Aren't pilgrims just people who move to a new place looking for freedom?

Mrs. O'Connor: That's right. Usually, pilgrims are looking for religous freedom, but anyone seeking freedom in a new land can be called a pilgrim.

Mario: America is made up of people who came from other places . . .

Karen: . . . or their parents or grandparents or great-grandparents came from other countries. Even Native Americans came to this land at one point in history, but that was many years ago.

The Thanksgiving Program (cont.)

Mrs. O'Connor: Right here in this class we have children whose ancestors came from Japan, Saudi Arabia, Africa, Brazil, and England, to name just a few.

Jeff: I was born across the ocean in Korea . . .

Mario: . . . and my parents and I came here from Mexico not long ago.

Mai Li: My older brother was born before my parents left China.

Sima: I still have several relatives living in India.

Nicholas: My parents are Italian and French. Italy and France are in Europe, you know.

Andy: My grandparents came to this country from Canada long before my parents were born.

Mrs. O'Connor: And my great-grandparents came here from Ireland and Scotland.

Lisa: Boy! Was I wrong when I said the only real Americans are people who were born here along with their parents.

Mrs. O'Connor: I think we've all learned a good lesson today. Let's write about what it means to be an American, and we can read our stories at our program next week.

Ben: And then can we have a feast?

Mrs. O'Connor: Yes, Ben, then we can have a feast.

Narrator 2:   The program was a huge success, and the parents were very proud of their children.

Narrator 3:   The children learned an important lesson they will never forget: It takes all kinds of people to make up a great nation like America.

Announcer: We hope you enjoyed our presentation of "The Thanksgiving Program."

Announcer: Our class will now recite a poem called "A Pilgrim of Today" and sing a song called "A Pilgrim Song." We hope you enjoy them.

Announcer: This is the end of our program. Thank you for being such good listeners.

Invitation

Please join us for our Readers' Theater presentation of

The Thanksgiving Program

Date: _____

Time: _____

Place: _____

Presented by: _____

Bibliography

Brown, Marc. *Arthur's Thanksgiving.* Little Brown, 1984.

Bunting, Eve. *How Many Days to America: A Thanksgiving Story.* Clarion Books, 1990.

Bunting, Eve. *The Wednesday Surprise.* Clarion Books, 1990.

Cohen, Barbara. *Molly's Pilgrim.* Lothrop, Lee & Shepard, 1983.

Higgins, Susan Olson. *The Thanksgiving Book.* Pumpkin Publishers, 1984.

Kroll, Steven. *Oh, What a Thanksgiving!* Scholastic, 1988.

Levinson, Riki. *Our Home Is the Sea.* Puffin, 1992.

Lyon, George Ella. *Came a Tide.* Orchard Books, 1990.

Prelutsky, Jack. *It's Thanksgiving.* Greenwillow, 1982.

Rylant, Cynthia. *The Relatives Came.* Macmillan Child Group, 1985.

Stanek, Muriel. *I Speak English for My Mother.* A. Whitman, 1989.

Stevenson, James. *Fried Feathers for Thanksgiving.* Greenwillow, 1986.

Waters, Kate. *Samuel Eaton's Day: A Day in the Life of a Pilgrim Boy.* Scholastic, 1993.

Waters, Kate. *Sarah Morton's Day: A Day in the Life of a Pilgrim Girl.* Scholastic, 1989.

Video

Brown, Jeff and Chris Pelzer (producers). *Molly's Pilgrim.* Phoenix Films, 1985. (This was an Academy Award winner for best live-action short film.)